THE 8 Other Advantages of Universal Life

TOM MARTIN

CFP®, CLU®, ChFC®

Printed in the United States of America

First Printing, 2015

ISBN 978-1-932860-05-4

Stellar Press
P.O. Box 300222
Saint Louis, MO 63130

Live as if you were to die tomorrow. Learn as if you were to live forever. - *Mahatma Gandhi*

Disclaimer

This book is intended to show some of the unique advantages of universal life insurance. Many of the concepts contained herein involve complex ideas that have been oversimplified as the full complexity may be beyond the scope of this book. It is further assumed, unless otherwise noted, that the permanent life insurance policies illustrated will be kept in force until death to preserve the tax-free benefits. This book is presented solely for educational and entertainment purposes. The author and publisher are not offering it as legal, accounting, tax or investment services advice. While best efforts have been used in preparing this book, the author and publisher make no representations or warranties of any kind and assume no liabilities of any kind with respect to the accuracy or completeness of the contents and specifically disclaim any implied warranties of merchantability or fitness of use for a particular purpose. Neither the author nor the publisher shall be held liable or responsible to any person or entity with respect to any loss or incidental or consequential damages caused, or alleged to have been caused, directly or indirectly, by the information or programs contained herein. You should consult with qualified advisors before implementing any of the ideas presented in this book.

Dedication

This book is dedicated to all of my clients whose individual circumstances have led me down a path of greater discovery about the many benefits of permanent life insurance.

The Eight Other Advantages of Universal Life

Table of Contents

The Eight Other Advantages of Universal Life

Forward

The true sign of intelligence is not knowledge
but imagination. - *Albert Einstein*

This book is written for life insurance advisors,
CPAs, attorneys, bankers, investment advisors,
business owners, and consumers to shed light on
the very complex and important subject of life
insurance planning. There is perhaps no more
maligned product in the financial world than permanent cash value life insurance, which includes
universal life, whole life, variable life, and equity
indexed universal life. The arguments against these
products seem to focus on only one aspect of permanent life insurance: the cash value.

We often hear permanent life insurance described
as term insurance with an investment component.
If this description were complete, the only question we would need to answer to make a good
decision is "Does the cash accumulation of this

policy justify the higher premium?" Unfortunately, this is where most agents, advisors, and consumers focus all of their analysis.

For the record, I am a believer in using life insurance as a cash accumulation vehicle. When balanced with other investment products and good planning, the versatility and tax advantages of cash value life insurance can offer great benefits. But cash value is only one of nine advantages of universal life. This book explains the eight advantages of universal life other than cash value.

In my examples I will use a very low premium, low cash value policy to get the issue of cash accumulation off the table from the start. Not all companies will offer plans with such low premiums and low accumulation values but these plans do exist. My intent in using such a plan in my examples is not to endorse this type of a plan over a higher premium plan with more cash accumulation. Instead, it is to focus the discussion on the other advantages.

While in my examples I will use equity indexed universal life (IUL), the concepts apply to traditional universal life, variable universal life, and, to a lesser extent, whole life.

Chapter 1

A New Prospect

There are worse things in life than death. Have you ever spent an evening with an insurance salesman? - *Woody Allen*

Monday morning my phone rings. It's my friend Fred Stone. "Tom, my banker said that I need to call you," he began. "I'm planning a fairly extensive expansion of my quarry, so I'm applying for a large line of credit at the bank. The banker says that I need to have life insurance in place to cover the loan in case something happens to me."

"How much life insurance is the bank requiring?" I asked.

"They want me to have $10,000,000 of coverage for at least 20 years," Fred replied.

I already know Fred is 50 years old, so I ask him to tell me about his health.

"Well, I'm a bit overweight," Fred replied. "My doctor told me to lose about 20 pounds and to start eating better to get my cholesterol and blood pressure down," he added. "But other than that, I guess I'm pretty healthy. Last time I bought life insurance I got standard rates, so I expect to get the same now," he said.

"Great," I responded. "I'll put some options together and we will discuss them next week."

When running quotes for a large life insurance purchase, especially with new coverage, I always start with term insurance to serve as a baseline for comparison. While I truly believe that universal life is almost always the better choice, it is important for the client to see the full range of options. Secondly, it is difficult to appreciate the advantages of the universal life policy without an understanding of the cost of the "pure protection" that term provides.

After talking with Fred, I go to my term quote engine that shops over 20 different companies to be sure that I am giving Fred the best possible rates. I also run an illustration for a low premium universal life to show as an alternative.

Chapter 2

Yellow Ball Corner Pocket

The pessimist complains about the wind; the optimist expects it to change; the realist adjusts the sails. - William Arthur Ward

When Fred and I meet two weeks after our conversation, we go over the options I assembled for him.

"Fred, assuming that you qualify for standard non-smoker rates, here are the three least expensive companies," I explained. "The reason that I'm showing three companies is that from an underwriting standpoint, you seem borderline for standard rates. I want to give you an idea of what kind of premium to expect if we are not able to get the standard rates for the cheapest company. At this point I am just going off the health information that you provided me. The insurance company will require a physical and they will also order records from your physicians. In that underwriting process they may need to adjust the premiums up or down. Since, at this point, we don't know what the final rates will be, for planning purposes we should assume the third lowest rate. Obviously, if we can get the lowest rate we would take that."

Below are the options I assembled for Fred.

$10,000,000 Twenty Year Term		
Fred Stone		
Male age 50 Standard Non-tobacco		
Company	Boulder Life	Dinosaur Life	Granite City Life
Financial Rating	A	A++	A+
Annual Premium	$30,400	$32,300	$33,000
Convertibility Age	65	70	70
Policy Termination	Age 70	Age 95	Age 95

"As you can see, Boulder Life is the lowest premium at $30,400," I told Fred. "Dinosaur Life is coming in at $32,300, and Granite City Life is $33,000," I added. "All are strong companies and, other than premium, the policies are all very similar. All policies can be converted to universal life. The Boulder policy would need to be converted by age 65 but the others can be converted up to age 70. It's also worth noting that the Boulder Life policy will terminate at age 70 and cannot be continued. The other policies can be renewed to age 95 but at substantially higher premiums."

"Great," said Fred. "Then let's apply with Boulder Life."

"Before doing that," I replied, "I want to go over an alternate strategy. Fred, do you ever play pool?"

"Sure, I've played before," Fred responded quizzically. "What does that have to do with life insurance?"

"In some ways life insurance planning is a lot like a billiards game," I explained. "Really anyone can play, the rules are fairly simple, and it doesn't take great skill to knock the cue ball into another ball. But, if we go to a pool hall it is easy to tell the 'hacks' from the more skilled players."

Fred looked at me somewhat confused about the change in topic.

I continued, "The hack will approach the table and identify the easiest shot: yellow ball, corner pocket. After taking that shot he will then approach the next shot in the same way until he gives up his turn to his opponent. The skilled player, on the other hand, will approach the table and first identify the easiest shot, in this case, yellow ball, corner pocket. But then he would ask himself, 'what kind of opportunities will I have after taking this shot?' Yellow ball, corner pocket is clearly the easiest shot, but red ball, side pocket is only slightly more difficult and it sets the player up so that he should be able to go green ball, corner pocket and then on to sink the yellow ball. Sometimes the easiest shot also turns out to be the best shot, but we never really know until we examine other shot combinations."

"I'm still wondering how this fits in to our discussion," Fred said.

"Fred, you'll surely have other financial needs, concerns, and opportunities that you'll need to address after making this financial decision on your life insurance," I answered. "While, right now, you are viewing the life insurance as simply something that the bank is requiring for your loan, it may play a part in financial matters down the road. What I showed you in the term quotes was the equivalent of yellow ball corner pocket. It represents the easiest shot because it is the cheapest way to address your immediate need, and maybe that is the shot you should take. But, I'd like to spend a little bit of time talking about financial concerns that you will have in the future to see if that truly represents the best shot to take," I added.

"Okay," Fred asked, "what do you have in mind?"

"I'd like to show you another option called universal life," I responded. "Bedrock Life has an equity index universal life (IUL) that may work very well in your situation."

"Stop right there," Fred boldly stated. "I have no interest in spending a lot more money to accumulate cash value. My financial advisor, Suze Boreman, says that cash value life insurance is the worst investment you can possibly make. And all of the financial people on the radio and TV seem to agree," he asserted. "You're much better off investing in a mutual fund or with a decent broker."

"Fred, bear with me," I said. I expected Fred to have this reaction, because there's so much misunderstanding about life insurance. "First off, I'm not talking about spending a lot more money nor am I talking about accumulating a lot of cash in the policy," I told him. "Universal life allows you to decide how much premium you want to pay, subject to limits. This policy from Bedrock Life happens to have a really low minimum premium— almost as low as term. But with universal life, there are a lot of benefits that you don't get with term. These benefits go well beyond the cash value of the policy, so let's take a look at the policy."

Since Fred brought up cash value, I begin there.

Chapter 3

Benefit 1: Cash Value

Price is what you pay. Value is what you get.
Warren Buffett

Cash value life insurance (universal life and whole life) is often described as term insurance with an "investment or savings component." If that were the only difference between permanent insurance and cash value insurance, the only question we would need to address would be whether the cash value of the policy justifies the increased premium. Volumes have been written on this topic, and I will not attempt to make an argument on either side.

Cash accumulation in a life insurance policy is certainly a benefit but certainly not the only benefit. Even if a policy, like the one we will be discussing, does an admittedly poor job of accumulating cash value, other benefits may indeed make the permanent policy a better buy.

I begin my discussion with Fred by showing him

the ledger of the Bedrock Indexed Universal Life policy.

Bedrock Life Indexed Universal Life				
Fred Stone Male age 50 Standard Non-tobacco				
Projected Values assuming 7% interest crediting				
Pol. Yr.	**Age**	**Premium**	**Cash Value**	**Death Benefit**
1	50	$42,000	$0	$10,000,000
2	51	$42,000	$0	$10,000,000
3	52	$42,000	$0	$10,000,000
4	53	$42,000	$0	$10,000,000
5	54	$42,000	$0	$10,000,000
6	55	$42,000	$543	$10,000,000
7	56	$42,000	$1,424	$10,000,000
8	57	$42,000	$3,258	$10,000,000
9	58	$42,000	$4,876	$10,000,000
10	59	$42,000	$6,736	$10,000,000
11	60	$42,000	$9,987	$10,000,000
12	61	$42,000	$14,521	$10,000,000
13	62	$42,000	$20,874	$10,000,000
14	63	$42,000	$30,795	$10,000,000
15	64	$42,000	$45,687	$10,000,000
16	65	$42,000	$63,876	$10,000,000
17	66	$42,000	$83,589	$10,000,000
18	67	$42,000	$105,976	$10,000,000
19	68	$42,000	$124,983	$10,000,000
20	69	$42,000	$140,321	$10,000,000
21	70	$42,000	$173,564	$10,000,000
22	71	$42,000	$143,560	$10,000,000
23	72	$42,000	$90,466	$10,000,000
24	73	$42,000	$48,596	$10,000,000
25	74	$42,000	$1,564	$10,000,000

"Here's a table that shows the premium and cash values of the Bedrock IUL," I told Fred. "As you can see, the annual premium is $42,000, which is more than the term insurance, but probably a lot less than what you may have been expecting when I brought up the idea of universal life."

"That's true," Fred replied. "Somebody tried to sell me universal life years ago and, as I recall, the premium was about five or six times what term was."

"That may be the case," I replied. "Most universal life policies that I see are run with much higher premiums in order to develop a lot of cash value. I know that in your case, Fred, cash accumulation is not a priority right now. I would imagine that money invested in your business at this point will certainly beat any investment you could consider. With that in mind, I designed this policy to keep the premium low and, as a result, the policy develops very little cash value. One of the advantages of universal life is a flexible premium structure. You have the ability to pay what you want within certain limits."

"What are the limits and who sets them?" Fred asked.

"The insurance company sets a minimum premium, and it differs from company to company and policy to policy. Typically the minimum premium is substantially higher than term insurance, but there are some policies that have minimum premiums close to term. Bedrock is one company that offers a term-like minimum premium," I explained.

"Why would an insurance company have a maximum premium?" Fred asked. "I wouldn't think you'd have an argument with a life insurance company if you wanted to pay more than what was required."

"The maximum premium is actually determined by the tax code. We'll talk about that a bit later."

I explain to Fred that the $42,000 premium is the minimum premium for this particular policy and at that premium level it will carry the policy about 25 years. Since we are paying such a low premium, Fred wouldn't expect to develop much cash value, but it does develop some.

"Tom, if I'm reading this right, it looks like there is no cash surrender value for the first five years, and even after 20 years, if I cashed the policy in, I would only get back about $140,000. Am I reading this right?" asked Fred.

"Yes, you are," I answered.

"Do you think I was born yesterday?!" Fred asked. "Over 20 years I will have spent $840,000 in premiums only to get back $140,000 20 years later! Why would anybody think that's a good deal?"

"Fred," I calmly replied, "first of all, you need to look at the marginal difference in cost. The $42,000 premium is only $9,000 more than the Granite City term policy. So, over 20 years, the Bedrock IUL will cost $180,000 more. But, if you cashed the policy in 20 years later and got back $140,000, on a net basis the universal life policy will only have cost $40,000 more. If you look at it on a net cost basis, it is really only about $2,000 per year more than the term."

"But Suze is right, that still is an awful investment!" Fred exclaimed. "Imagine how much money I would have if I simply invested that $9,000 per year cost difference. Surely it would be a lot more than $140,000! You're telling me that this is a good deal?"

"Yes," I said evenly, with a smile. This is a common reaction. "It is a good deal, but not because of the cash value. If the only difference between term and universal life was the cash component, I would be the first to admit that this is not a good deal. But this is a universal life policy, and it comes with all kinds of additional benefits other than cash value. I think you'll see that those benefits are worth the relatively small difference in net cost."

I continued, "Fred, over 20 years this policy will cost you about 25% more than the Granite City term on a gross basis. And on a net basis, after accounting for the cash surrender value, it's only about 6% more, right?" I asked.

"Well, yes," replied Fred. "But it is still more. Why would I want to pay more?"

"Term insurance basically just provides protection against premature death," I explained. "Cash value policies, specifically universal life, provide that protection as well as many others. It's not just about the cash value. And, admittedly, in this policy, I'm showing you that cash value certainly is not all that advantageous. As a matter of fact, I could not possibly craft an argument that you should buy this policy based on its cash value alone. Now, let's talk about the eight other benefits of universal life."

With the argument of cash value off the table, I am now able to proceed to a discussion on the eight other advantages of universal life.

Chapter 4

Benefit 2: Lapse Protection

*It is always wise to look ahead, but difficult to
look further than you can see.*
Winston Churchill

"Fred, every month I get a couple of notices of
clients who are late on their life insurance. It can
happen even to the most responsible people who
always pay their other bills on time. Sometimes, it's
a problem with the mail. Sometimes premiums are
missed because the insured is out of town. Or perhaps the person simply forgot to pay," I explained
to Fred. "The insurance company does allow a
grace period but once that is up they may refuse to
renew the policy unless you give them proof that
you are still healthy," I added.

I continued, "One of the benefits of universal life
is that the extra premium you pay goes into an account in your policy, and that account is available
to pay any missed premiums. The account value
is normally sufficient to sustain your policy for
months or even years after a premium is missed."

I added. "I know this doesn't sound like a big benefit but potentially it could be worth the entire $10 million face amount of the policy if it protects you from inadvertently lapsing the policy."

"Just last month I had a situation that illustrates this benefit. I sold a rather large policy to my client Randy. Randy was in excellent health and purchased a 20 year term policy at preferred plus rates. His annual premium was just below $5,000. At his first anniversary, I received a notice that he did not pay the premium, so I called him. I explained to him that he needed to send in his money by the end of the grace period. The insurance company received the check the day before the grace period expired. Unfortunately, this pattern continued every year until this year."

"What happened this year?" Fred inquired.

"I reminded him about the premium and the grace period. He said he was leaving town but would leave a check with his secretary. He ended up leaving without signing the check. I was able to reach him by phone and he said that he would sign when he got back in town but that was after the grace period. I told him that he would need to complete a form showing that there was no change in health. He said he was healthy so that would not be a problem."

"So what happened?"

"The insurance company ordered updated medical records. And it turns out there was a change in his health. He had put on a little weight and was being treated for high blood pressure, but the biggest problem was that he was now being treated for sleep apnea. The insurance company refused to renew the policy. We ended up having to buy a new policy from a different insurer and the policy was rated for sleep apnea."

"How much more did that cost him?" asked Fred.

"His premium went from just under $5,000 to a little over $16,000. That $11,000 mistake will be compounded over the next 15 years. I looked back into my files when I sold him the initial term policy and I was reminded that I had also proposed a universal life for a premium of $10,000. Even though the universal life wouldn't have had much cash surrender value, the $35,000 account value would have been sufficient to keep the policy alive for six or seven years without any further premiums."

"Tom," Fred said confidently, "I pay all my bills on time so I really don't see much benefit in that. Certainly not enough to justify the difference in annual premium."

"I agree with you," I replied. "If you pay your bills on time, the benefit alone does not justify that much more premium but it is still a nice safety net to have. Let's talk about the next benefit."

Chapter 5

Benefit 3: Long Term Care Benefit

Don't be afraid to see what you see.
Ronald Reagan

"Fred, many of today's universal life policies offer early access to the policy's death benefit if the insured needs long-term care," I explained. "Not all policies offer this, but the Bedrock universal life policy features this benefit. That means if you suffered an accident, sickness, or injury that required long-term care, Bedrock will allow you to withdraw up to 2% of your death benefit each month until 95% of the policy is exhausted. This benefit is capped at the IRS per diem max, which is currently about $10,000 per month," I added. "Since 2% of $10 million is much more than the $10,000 cap, your benefit would be the maximum of $10,000 per month. And, since the IRS limit is indexed for inflation, your benefit would increase each year by the inflation rate."

Fred nodded. "I know long-term care can be expensive," he added. "After my Dad had a stroke he needed to stay in a nursing home for a few months and then he needed in-home care for the next few years until he died. I was surprised to learn that these expenses were not covered by Medicare. Fortunately, he did have a lot of money, but I know my Mom was very worried about running out of money and she probably would have if Dad were still alive today."

"Fred, if you were in the market for a long-term care policy offering a lifetime inflation adjusted monthly benefit of $10,000 per month, the premium would likely be about $12,000 per year," I said. "In your case, you would be picking up this benefit by just spending an extra $2,000 per year in net cost."

"Tom, some of my friends have purchased long-term care insurance, but frankly I've always thought that this is something that older people do," admitted Fred. "Maybe we can talk about that need in a few years. If I were in the market for both long-term care and life insurance, I guess this would be a pretty good deal. But right now I just want to address the life insurance side of it. And I'd like to do it as cheaply as possible."

Fred certainly saw more value in the long-term care benefit than in the lapse protection benefit but I could tell he was mostly concerned with cost containment. Fred has a lot of things on his plate with his business expansion plans. He wants to make good decisions and can afford to make better long-term decisions when they make sense.

Admittedly, the chances of somebody Fred's age triggering the long-term care benefit in the next 20 years are relatively small, so we will move on to the next point.

Chapter 6

Benefit 4: Continuability

The ultimate test of man's conscience may be his willingness to sacrifice something today for future generations whose words of thanks will not be heard. - *Gaylord Nelson*

"Fred, I want to point something out on the term proposals. If you wanted to renew the term beyond the 20-year time frame the premiums will be substantially higher. The Boulder term does not allow you an option to renew after age 70. Both Dinosaur and Granite City allow renewals up to age 95, but at a substantially higher premium."

Term Premiums After Age 70			
Age	Boulder Life	Dinosaur Life	Granite City Life
70	NA	$364,069	$384,256
71		$398,529	$401,250
72		$427,263	$429,042
73		$463,669	$474,542
74		$514,469	$516,259

Age	Boulder Life	Dinosaur Life	Granite City Life
75		$601,669	$603,266
76		$699,645	$710,015
77		$724,869	$826,452
78		$851,058	$905,052
89		$989,543	$1,115,231
80		$1,251,546	$1,355,144
81		$1,499,848	$1,501,522
82		$1,682,869	$1,745,899
83		$2,460,459	$2,280,859
84		$3,481,459	$3,619,366

Fred's eyes widen. "Is that a misprint or does the premium really jump to $364,000?" he asked.

"No, it's not a misprint," I said. "It does rise to that level, and then it goes to $398,000 the next year and keeps going up."

"Who in their right mind would pay that?"

"Well, if you were deathly ill you may indeed be willing to pay that," I explained. "The insurance company has to assume that if people want to carry their insurance longer than the term they elected, chances are that they've had a change in health. Insurance companies figure that if the person decided they still wanted life insurance then they would have searched the market for the most competitive premium. If they were healthy enough to get approved by another company, they would not be renewing their current policy," I continued. "Therefore the company assumes that anybody renewing beyond 20 years is seriously ill, and that's one of the reasons that the premium is so high."

"Well, I certainly won't need this coverage for more than 20 years," stated Fred. "By age 70, I will have sold my business, and the bank would not be requiring the coverage."

"Fred, as you can imagine, in my 25 years in business, I've sold quite a few term policies. One thing that I have found in common with all of my term clients is that when their term comes to an end, they always inquire about what it will cost to continue it," I said. "Some are interested in continuing it for a period of just a few years, and others may want to continue it indefinitely. But virtually all of them are at least interested in seeing options to continue coverage."

"Do they really pay those obscene rates?" Fred asked.

"Mostly not," I answered. "I have had at least two clients, however, who have renewed their policies beyond the term period," I said. "In both cases, these clients had been recently diagnosed with cancer and felt they had a short life expectancy. They just didn't want to lose their coverage at such a critical time. One of them died about a year later and, in retrospect, his decision to continue the insurance, even at an exorbitant premium, was a good decision. The other continued to pay the higher premium for about three years. After that, his cancer went into remission, and he decided to discontinue the policy. Even though it turned out that continuing the policy did not pay off for him, he didn't regret his decision of continuing it for a few years."

"Another thing that I've learned throughout my career in helping people with their finances is that life never works out exactly the way we plan it," I told Fred. "I've worked with plenty of young professionals who were absolutely sure they would not need life insurance for more than 15 or 20 years, only to find themselves buying much larger policies later," I said. "They may have expanded their business, and the bank requires larger policies to cover larger bank loans. Or maybe they're earning a lot more money now and aren't ready to retire because their lifestyle has grown with their income. Or maybe their income protection needs have been replaced with estate planning needs," I explain.

"Fred, at this point, the estate planning that you've done has been primarily focused on taking care of your family in the event of your death," I continued. "Twenty years from now, after you've sold your business and entered your advanced years, your estate planning will be more focused on how to most efficiently transfer the wealth you've accumulated to the people or organizations you care about," I said. "In that case, I suspect your view of life insurance may change from a protection-oriented vehicle to a wealth-transfer vehicle. I believe that 20 years from now, there is a very good chance that you will be interested in exploring the possibilities of continuing your life insurance coverage," I stated.

Fred nodded his head in agreement.

"I would shy away from the Boulder policy simply for its limited ability to be continued. You could convert it to universal life but you would need to make that decision by age 65. The other two policies allow for conversion up to age 70," I explained.

"In rare cases does it make sense to renew a term policy beyond its level period," I explained. "Normally if coverage is desired in later years, universal life is the better choice because, unlike term, it is designed to be kept until death."

"Let me give you an idea of the cost structure on the Dinosaur Life or Granite City Life if you decided to convert them at age 70," I continued. "Dinosaur Life has a pretty competitive universal life policy. If a 70-year-old converted his coverage today the annual premium would be about $400,000 for a $10 million policy. At that premium level the policy would provide coverage to age 98. You could pay a little more to extend coverage beyond that point or slightly less premium but the policy would not last quite that long. The Granite City universal life has a similar cost structure," I said.

Dinosaur Life Universal Life				
Male age 70 Standard Non-tobacco				
Term Conversion				
			Projected Values assuming 7% interest crediting	
Pol. Yr.	Age	Premium	Cash Value	Death Benefit
20	70	$401,276	$0	$10,000,000
21	71	$401,276	$54,596	$10,000,000
22	72	$401,276	$105,264	$10,000,000
23	73	$401,276	$168,256	$10,000,000
24	74	$401,276	$221,543	$10,000,000
25	75	$401,276	$315,491	$10,000,000
26	76	$401,276	$515,644	$10,000,000
27	77	$401,276	$845,645	$10,000,000
28	78	$401,276	$1,204,877	$10,000,000

Pol. Yr.	Age	Premium	Cash Value	Death Benefit
29	79	$401,276	$1,645,487	$10,000,000
30	80	$401,276	$2,048,871	$10,000,000
31	81	$401,276	$2,254,875	$10,000,000
32	82	$401,276	$2,356,484	$10,000,000
33	83	$401,276	$2,354,651	$10,000,000
34	84	$401,276	$2,315,468	$10,000,000
35	85	$401,276	$2,298,745	$10,000,000
36	86	$401,276	$2,197,426	$10,000,000
37	87	$401,276	$2,000,978	$10,000,000
38	88	$401,276	$1,818,768	$10,000,000
39	89	$401,276	$1,604,890	$10,000,000
40	90	$401,276	$1,416,584	$10,000,000

Fred interjected, "Why couldn't I just buy another term policy at age 70 if I wanted to continue coverage?"

"You possibly could," I answered, "as long as you remain healthy. But a lot can change in your health between now and then. If you remain a standard risk, based on today's rates, a 10-year term policy on a 70-year-old would cost about $20 per $1,000 of coverage. So a $10 million term would cost about $200,000. Of course, you would end up facing the same dilemma at age 80. Most people who are still considering life insurance in their later years opt for universal life so they can keep the coverage until they die."

"The premium I am showing on the Bedrock universal life policy is only sufficient to keep the policy in force for about 25 years but you can increase the premiums at any time to carry the policy longer," I said. "Suppose you wanted to continue your coverage to age 73. At age 70, the cash value is projected to be $140,000. At that point you could stop paying premium and the policy will feed off of its cash value for three years before it runs out of value. So, the cost of carrying the policy for three additional years would be the $140,000 cash value that you would have lost. By comparison, a term policy, assuming you remain healthy, would cost about $200,000 a year. In this case, the Bedrock UL would have saved you nearly $500,000!" I exclaimed.

Bedrock Life Indexed Universal Life				
Fred Stone Male age 50 Standard Non-tobacco				
			Projected Values assuming 7% interest crediting	
Pol. Yr.	Age	Premium	Cash Value	Death Benefit
1	50	$42,000	$0	$10,000,000
2	51	$42,000	$0	$10,000,000
3	52	$42,000	$0	$10,000,000
4	53	$42,000	$0	$10,000,000
5	54	$42,000	$0	$10,000,000
6	55	$42,000	$543	$10,000,000

Pol. Yr.	Age	Premium	Cash Value	Death Benefit
7	56	$42,000	$1,424	$10,000,000
8	57	$42,000	$3,258	$10,000,000
9	58	$42,000	$4,876	$10,000,000
10	59	$42,000	$6,736	$10,000,000
11	60	$42,000	$9,987	$10,000,000
12	61	$42,000	$14,521	$10,000,000
13	62	$42,000	$20,874	$10,000,000
14	63	$42,000	$30,795	$10,000,000
15	64	$42,000	$45,687	$10,000,000
16	65	$42,000	$63,876	$10,000,000
17	66	$42,000	$83,589	$10,000,000
18	67	$42,000	$105,976	$10,000,000
19	68	$42,000	$124,983	$10,000,000
20	69	$42,000	$140,321	$10,000,000
21	70	$0	$131,512	$10,000,000
22	71	$0	$98,548	$10,000,000
23	72	$0	$45,600	$10,000,000
24	73	$0	Lapse	$0

"Now let's assume that you were interested in continuing your coverage forever," I continued. "Converting either of the term policies would cost about $400,000 per year." I said.

"By comparison, if you wanted to extend coverage on the Bedrock UL policy to age 100 it would only cost about $150,000 per year," I added. "Fred, if you died at age 80, the Bedrock UL policy would have saved you about $2.5 million in premium. At age 90, the savings would be about $5 million by continuing the Bedrock policy versus buying term now and converting later," I explained.

Bedrock Life Indexed Universal Life				
Fred Stone Male age 50 Standard Non-tobacco				
			Projected Values assuming 7% interest crediting	
Pol. Yr.	Age	Premium	Cash Value	Death Benefit
20	70	$42,000	$140,321	$10,000,000
21	71	$150,000	$300,568	$10,000,000
22	72	$150,000	$462,486	$10,000,000
23	73	$150,000	$624,658	$10,000,000
24	74	$150,000	$825,645	$10,000,000
25	75	$150,000	$1,008,904	$10,000,000
26	76	$150,000	$1,254,894	$10,000,000
27	77	$150,000	$1,518,456	$10,000,000
28	78	$150,000	$1,789,045	$10,000,000
29	79	$150,000	$2,015,484	$10,000,000
30	80	$150,000	$2,354,651	$10,000,000
31	81	$150,000	$2,694,518	$10,000,000
32	82	$150,000	$3,159,485	$10,000,000
33	83	$150,000	$3,354,658	$10,000,000
34	84	$150,000	$3,645,841	$10,000,000
35	85	$150,000	$3,948,542	$10,000,000
36	86	$150,000	$4,484,548	$10,000,000
37	87	$150,000	$4,615,424	$10,000,000

Pol. Yr.	Age	Premium	Cash Value	Death Benefit
38	88	$150,000	$4,701,514	$10,000,000
39	89	$150,000	$4,645,154	$10,000,000
40	90	$150,000	$4,487,818	$10,000,000
50	100	$150,000	$658,987	$10,000,000

"There is an enormous amount of savings in the future just by paying a little bit more now," I further added.

"Hmmm." Fred is somewhat interested, but he doesn't see how this ties into his long-term strategy. "Tom, as I've said, by age 70 I will have plenty of money and will not need the insurance. When I die, my kids are going to get plenty of money. I really don't see why I would want to spend my money in retirement just to make my kids even richer when I die. The fact is that I am not a huge fan of life insurance now. I doubt that I will be a bigger fan 20 years from now, especially with the premiums that you just showed me," Fred said.

Chapter 7

Benefit 5: Salability

Someday I want to be rich. Some people get so rich they lose all respect for humanity. That's how rich I want to be. - Rita Rudner

"Fred, you seem awfully certain that you will not want to carry the insurance beyond age 70," I said.

"Certainly not at those premiums," he replied. "Maybe if I'm on my deathbed, but short of that I really cannot see myself paying premiums like that."

"Cashing in a universal life policy is not your only exit strategy. One of the exit options for universal life, which is generally not available with term, is selling the policy as a life settlement," I told him.

"About 20 years ago, a new industry emerged called the life settlement industry," I told Fred. "Life settlement companies buy life insurance policies from people who no longer want them. The way it works is that investors pool their money to buy these policies. They take over ownership of the policies, pay all the premiums, and collect the death benefits upon death. The good news is that what they pay you for your policy is always significantly larger than what you would get by cashing the policy in."

I told Fred that the price they will pay depends on a variety of factors including:

- The insured's health and life expectancy at the time of settlement (the more unhealthy the insured is, the greater the price).
- How much premium is required to keep the coverage in force to death.
- Overall market conditions.

"I've done a handful of life settlements in my career," I explained. "The offers have ranged from about 5% of the face value of the policy to about 30%," I said. "In your case, using these ranges, your policy may be worth between $500,000 and $3,000,000 in the settlement market. That's much higher than what you would receive by cashing in the policy."

"Can term policies be settled?" Fred asked.

"Technically, yes," I told him. "But they generally need to be converted to universal life first. As we discussed, it will be much more expensive to convert a term policy to a universal life policy than to simply continue an existing universal life. The increased cost of the conversion policy relative to the Bedrock policy may mean the difference between getting an offer and not getting an offer," I explained.

"I've read about life settlements and the whole idea sounds kind of morbid," Fred said.

"Initially that was my reaction too," I confessed. "But the more of them I see, the more comfortable I am with the idea. I initially found the industry to be predatory, taking advantage of other people's health problems," I continued. "But if the insured valued the coverage more than the money they would receive as a settlement, they would just keep the coverage. On the other hand, if they valued cash in hand now, more than death benefit in the future, they would take the cash now. It is actually empowering to the insured because it gives them options they wouldn't otherwise have," I said.

"Fred, suppose 20 years from now you could sell your Bedrock universal life policy in the settlement market for $1.5 million," I said. "Would it be worth paying $9,000 more in annual premium for 20 years to end up with $1.5 million?"

"Sure it would," he responded.

"Well," I said, "this gets even better. You wouldn't pay tax on the full $1.5 million. The first $840,000 is completely income tax free, since your cost basis in the policy is $840,000. After taxes you would net over $1,200,000," I said. "If instead of spending the extra money on the Bedrock universal life, suppose you had just given that $9,000 per year to Suze Boreman to invest. What do you think she would need to earn on your money to achieve $1,200,000 after taxes in 20 years?" I asked him.

"I have no idea."

"Assuming a 40% tax rate," I said, "your money would need to earn about 26% every year for 20 years. "Has Suze ever been able to generate that kind of return for you?" I said, now smiling big.

"Well, certainly not year after year," Fred admitted. "But there's no guarantee that my policy will be worth $1.5 million in 20 years."

"No, there's not," I said. "But it could be worth even more. Then again, you may be too young and too healthy to get an offer at all," I said. "Frankly, right now the market is somewhat soft for settlements, and a lot of 70-year-olds are too healthy to get viable offers. But suppose there is even just a

10% chance of your policy being worth $1.5 million. Would it be worth spending an extra $9,000 per year?" I challenged him. "Remember that even if there is no settlement value, you would receive at least your cash value, again making the premium only $2,000 more on a net basis. I would say that's a pretty good trade off."

"Well, those odds seem better than what I would get in Vegas," he conceded.

"Fred, I wouldn't want you to go with the Bedrock UL policy just because of the ability to sell it, because that may or may not be an option for you," I said. "But this is a very strong advantage that universal life has over term that should definitely factor into your decision process."

Chapter 8

Benefit 6: The Ultimate Tax Haven

I want it said of me by those who knew me best, that I always plucked a thistle and planted a flower where I thought a flower would grow.
Abraham Lincoln

This is the longest chapter in the book, and for good reason: This benefit is the single greatest benefit of universal life. Yet it is rarely utilized. I've often wondered why, and I think it's because most advisors simply have no idea of the power of this benefit. But I want to communicate it to you, so let's pick up with my conversation with Fred.

"Fred, let's assume that you bought the Bedrock universal life policy, and everything went as you planned," I said. "You weren't late on premiums, so the lapse protection feature turned out to be of no value. You remained healthy, so the long-term care benefit was never triggered. You were able to sell your business for a handsome profit, and you retired a very wealthy man with no need or desire to carry life insurance into your future. You tried to sell the policy as a life settlement but your life expectancy was just too long to get a viable offer."

"In that case I guess I would just cash the policy in for $140,000 right?" asked Fred.

"Let's get away from the life insurance for a moment," I told him. "How much do you think you would have sold the business for?" I asked.

"Today, I think it is worth about $10 million," Fred answered. "I think it will be worth at least that much 20 years from now. I would say $15 million would certainly be a conservative figure."

"Would you expect that you'd be able to sell the business for cash?"

"Well, most of the people that I know who have sold their businesses are not able to get a full cash deal," Fred said. "They normally get a big percentage as cash and have to take installment payments on the balance. It's really not a bad way to go because it provides an income stream during the retirement years and spreads out some of the capital gain taxes."

"So let's assume that you sell the business 20 years from now for $15 million," I said. "You take $11 million as a cash payment and take back a 15-year note for the balance of $4 million. The $4 million note that you would take back would pay you about $400,000 for 15 years."

"I would be happy with that," Fred said.

"Let's talk about what you are going to do with the $11 million cash," I told him. "First you would have to pay capital gains taxes of about $3.3 million. That leaves about $7.7 million. A lot of my clients like to buy vacation homes after they sell their business and retire. Do you and your wife have any desire to do this?"

"We've always enjoyed the mountains and have talked about buying a place there once we retire."

"Okay, let's plan on earmarking $3.5 million for your mountain getaway."

"That sounds like a lot!" Fred shot back.

"You have to account for inflation," I explained. "If we assume real estate prices will inflate at 4% annually that would translate to about $1.5 million today. Obviously, that will be a nice house, but certainly within your means. Are there any other capital expenditures you'd like to plan for?"

"After cutting a check to Uncle Sam for $3.3 million and then another $3.5 million for my mountain home, I think I'd be done spending for a while. I guess I would give the rest to Suze Boreman to invest," he said.

"Tell me about the types of investments you would choose," I asked.

"Well, I'm pretty conservative when it comes to money. I don't handle market volatility well, and I doubt I will get any better as I get older," Fred replied. "I would imagine we'd put together a portfolio of diversified mutual funds. I would probably have about 2/3 in stocks and 1/3 in bonds. I'd probably balance more toward bonds as I get older."

"A portfolio like that would historically perform at a rate of 7%-8%," I commented.

"I would certainly be happy with that, but that would be on the high end of my expectations." Fred replied.

"How much income do you think you would need to draw out of that investment account?" I asked.

"I doubt I would need to take any income," Fred answered. "Between my 401k, social security, and the installment payments from my business sale,

I'm sure that I will have more than enough," he added. "I would imagine that I will just let my money grow."

"How long will you need to grow the money before you'll need to turn on an income stream?" I asked.

"I doubt I will ever need it," Fred answered. "As I said, my income picture looks pretty good. But if I want the money, I want to be able to get my hands on it at any time," he stated.

"So if you are going to grow it without ever dipping into it, what ultimately do you see happening to that money?" I prodded further.

"Well, I guess I will just die with it and leave it to my wife and kids," he answered.

"How much money do you think you will need to leave your wife and kids?" I responded.

Fred at this point was becoming a bit annoyed by this line of questioning. "I don't feel like I need to leave my kids anything. But I want them to have a good inheritance. I think I know where you're going with this," he continued. "You're going to tell me that if I plan on not spending my money and just eventually leave it to my kids, I'd be better off paying those outrageous life insurance premiums in order to continue the policy," he said.

"No, Fred, that really wasn't where I was going," I countered. "But we might as well talk about that idea."

"Here's the thing, Tom, I'm happy that I will leave my kids money, and I guess I want them to get as much as possible but not at my expense." Fred stated. "But this is my money we're talking about. It represents a lifetime of my hard work, my sacrifices, and my risk-taking. As long as I am alive, I want that money to be available to me! The kids will get what's left over, and it should be a great deal of money either way. Call me selfish, but that's just the way I feel!"

"No, I don't find that selfish at all," I assured him. "And my rather obnoxious line of questioning was meant to illustrate a point."

"What do you mean," Fred asked.

"When we've been talking about your life insurance, you've been using the word need. That is understandable because the insurance is needed to get your bank loan, which is needed to expand your business and that is why we are having this conversation. But when we talk about your money, you tend to focus not on needs but wants."

"Okay," Fred replied, curious as to where this conversation is headed.

"I also would prefer to talk about wants rather than needs; it makes for a more upbeat discussion."

"Fred," I continued, "you seem very certain about the things you think you will want in your retirement. You want to grow your money, you want to have access to your money under your terms, and you want your money to eventually transfer to your kids, as efficiently as possible."

"That sums it up pretty well," Fred responded, "especially the first two points!"

"And there are a few things I also picked up on that you definitely do not want" I added. "You don't seem to like the idea of paying more taxes than you need to, you don't like market volatility, and you definitely don't want to pay those 'outrageously high' life insurance premiums."

"You've got that right!" Fred exclaimed.

"Let's look at how your plan of investing that money with Suze Boreman would look like. We'll assume that you give her the $4.2 million after-tax amount from selling your business. And we'll further assume that she earns 8% each year, which is the high end of your expectation. Fred, what kind of fee does Suze charge to manage your money?"

"One percent," Fred said "that seems to be what everyone charges these days."

"Okay, we'll subtract her fee each year, and we will also need to subtract taxes. Some investment income is taxed at lower rates than ordinary income. In your case, I would assume that your investment income is taxed at a rate of 40%."

"That's a lot of tax. What about tax-free bonds or tax-deferred vehicles?" Fred asked.

"Tax-deferred vehicles do not eliminate the tax, they just postpone the tax." I explained. "Tax-free bonds, on the other hand, are income-tax-free, but the return is substantially lower than the 8% that we are projecting. You would likely net more money after taxes by investing at 8% taxable versus 3%-4% tax free. But I do like the fact that you are thinking in terms of net return."

"Fred, this spreadsheet shows how your $4.2 million would grow after fees and taxes if Suze were able to get an 8% return each year."

Year	Balance	Interest	Fee	Taxes	Net
1	$4,200,000	$336,000	$42,000	$117,600	$4,376,400
2	$4,376,400	$350,112	$43,764	$122,539	$4,560,209
3	$4,560,209	$364,817	$45,602	$127,686	$4,751,738
4	$4,751,738	$380,139	$47,517	$133,049	$4,951,311
5	$4,951,311	$396,105	$49,513	$138,637	$5,159,266
6	$5,159,266	$412,741	$51,593	$144,459	$5,375,955
7	$5,375,955	$430,076	$53,760	$150,527	$5,601,745
8	$5,601,745	$448,140	$56,017	$156,849	$5,837,018
9	$5,837,018	$466,961	$58,370	$163,437	$6,082,173
10	$6,082,173	$486,574	$60,822	$170,301	$6,337,624
11	$6,337,624	$507,010	$63,376	$177,453	$6,603,804
12	$6,603,804	$528,304	$66,038	$184,907	$6,881,164
13	$6,881,164	$550,493	$68,812	$192,673	$7,170,173
14	$7,170,173	$573,614	$71,702	$200,765	$7,471,320
15	$7,471,320	$597,706	$74,713	$209,197	$7,785,116
16	$7,785,116	$622,809	$77,851	$217,983	$8,112,091
17	$8,112,091	$648,967	$81,121	$227,139	$8,452,798
18	$8,452,798	$676,224	$84,528	$236,678	$8,807,816
19	$8,807,816	$704,625	$88,078	$246,619	$9,177,744
20	$9,177,744	$734,220	$91,777	$256,977	$9,563,209
Total			$1,276,955	$3,575,473	

"The good news is that over 20 years you would have more than doubled your money. But the bad news is that you would have paid nearly $5 million in fees and taxes."

"Those taxes and fees really add up. Suze and Uncle Sam together are taking about half of my earnings. But I think I found a mistake," Fred observed. "Suze's fee is only 1%, but it seems like her fee is about 1/3 of the tax due. How is this possible when the tax rate is 40 times higher than her fee?"

"The investment advisory fee," I explained, "applies to all of the money in the account, while the taxes apply only to the annual earnings of the account. So when we think about paying 1%, it seems small compared to a 40% rate. But in reality it does really eat into your savings."

I continued, "Fred let's evaluate this in terms of your goals of growing your money, having access to your money, and leaving what's left to your kids. Over 20 years your money would have doubled. Would that have met your goal of growing your money?"

"Well, yeah, I guess."

"At the end of the first year, how much money would you be able to get your hands on if you needed it?" I asked.

"Well, I assume I could get all of it if I need to. If your numbers are right, I'd have about $4.3 million."

"And," I continued, "what kind of inheritance would you leave your kids if you died that year, assuming you didn't spend anything from the account?"

"I imagine the kids would get the $4.3 million balance, right?"

"Exactly," I stated. "At all times you would have access to whatever is in the account after fees and taxes. And your kids will get whatever is left in the account at your death. Now how much will you have at age 80?"

"It looks like about $6.3 million."

"Yes," I replied "and that is also the amount you would leave to your kids if you died that year. Finally, what do those number look like at age 90?"

"About $9.5 million if I make it that long," replied Fred.

"I would say this would have done an adequate job of achieving the things you would want in an investment," I stated. "Your money would have grown, you would have maintained access to it, and whatever was left over would pass to your kids. It does also have a few things that you don't want. A portfolio consisting of 2/3 equities would have some volatility and, of course, you will be paying substantial taxes and fees. But at least you won't have any life insurance premiums to pay."

"Fred," I continued, "if we could reduce or eliminate the fees and taxes, your money would grow more quickly. If there was a way to do this while still maintaining the ability to access your money at any time under your own terms, would you want to know about it?"

"Absolutely!" Fred replied.

"Now, Fred, this may get a bit technical," I warned. "Remember when I said that with universal life you decide how much premium you want to pay subject to certain limits? The reason your Bedrock universal life policy has such a low premium and low cash values is that we are funding it with the minimum premium allowed by the insurance company. But there is also a maximum premium that is allowed. And you'll recall that I said that limit is set by the tax code."

"You may wonder why the IRS has an interest in how much life insurance premium you pay," I continued. "The reason is that they give very beneficial tax treatment to life insurance. Whenever the tax code gives us a benefit, it tends to want to limit how much we can use it," I added.

"Kind of like how I am capped on how much I can contribute to my 401k," Fred said.

"That's a great example," I said. "Suppose you were limited to a $50,000 contribution to your 401k this year, and you chose not to contribute. Could you then double the contribution next year?"

"No," Fred answered. "I asked my accountant that very question a few years ago."

"That's because the cap on retirement contributions is non-cumulative," I explained. "But unlike retirement contributions, the cap on life insurance premiums is cumulative. Any year you do not make the maximum contribution, whatever excess there is rolls into the next year, and it keeps rolling."

"What does this have to do with my investing?" Fred asked.

"As I said, the minimum premium for the Bedrock universal policy is $42,000 per year," I reminded him. "But the maximum that the tax code allows you to contribute over 20 years is approximately $300,000 per year. That means that over 20 years you are allowed to put about $6 million in premiums into that policy."

"Tom," Fred immediately interjected. "If you are

suggesting that I pay a premium of $300,000 a year into an insurance policy we can end this meeting right now!"

"No, I'm not suggesting that at all," I assured him. "Frankly, at this point in time, I agree that your money is best spent in your business."

"I am suggesting that you pay the minimum required premium of $42,000. Over 20 years you will have only put in $840,000 against your limit of nearly $6 million. That means that after year 20 you could put in an additional $5,160,000 without corrupting its tax treatment. What I am suggesting is that, rather than giving $4.2 million to Suze to invest, you may just want to put it into your policy."

"Are you kidding?" Fred asked. "Why would I do that?"

"You said you were interested in growing your money as quickly as possible, with full access to it any time you wanted the money," I answered. "You also wanted to minimize your taxes and leave whatever you don't spend to your children as efficiently as possible," I added. "The life insurance policy will do all of that. And it will do it much more efficiently than taxable mutual funds."

I showed Fred the policy illustration. "Let me show you what happens when you add $4.2 million in year 21," I started. "The $4.2 million earns the interest rate that the policy is crediting. I am assuming 7%, which is less than what we are assuming your funds would earn with Suze. But unlike the funds you would have had with Suze, no taxes are due on the earnings in the life insurance policy. Even though the policy is earning slightly less than Suze's investment, since there are no taxes, your cash value will grow more rapidly than it would in a taxable account earning 8%," I explained.

"Does the policy actually earn 7%?" Fred inquired.

"This policy's earnings are indexed to the S&P 500 so the actual crediting will vary from year to year," I explained. "It is guaranteed to earn at least 2% interest every year but it can earn up to 12% in any given year. Had you purchased this policy 20 years ago, you would have averaged a little over 8%. Over that last 20 years you probably would not have averaged that in the mutual fund portfolio that we discussed earlier. In other words, I am intentionally handicapping this comparison in favor of the mutual fund strategy. That's how powerful this is!"

"Fred, in repurposing your life insurance to act as an investment, the first thing we do is cut your death benefit down to the minimum. In this case we would cut if from $10 million to about $7.5 million. This is to minimize the charges that the insurance company takes from the cash value in order to cover their risk. In your case, the lowest we can go is $7.5 million. If we cut it any further we would lose the tax advantages. Next we put in the $4.2 million from your business sale."

Fred interrupted, "Not that I'm on board with this, but could I put in more money or less money?"

"As I said, you can put in up to $5,160,000, but if you did that much we would not be able to cut the death benefit down to the $7.5 million; we would have to keep it at $10 million. If you chose to do less," I continued, "we would cut the death benefit further. To make an even comparison, let's assume you did $4.2 million just like we assumed with the mutual fund portfolio."

"Fair enough," he replied.

I showed Fred the second page of the illustration showing the $4.2 million being paid in in year 21.

Bedrock Life Indexed Universal Life

Fred Stone Male age 50 Standard Non-tobacco

Pol. Yr.	Age	Premium	Projected Values assuming 7% interest crediting	
			Cash Value	Death Benefit
20	70	$42,000	$140,321	$10,000,000
21	71	$4,200,000	$4,377,911	$7,500,000
22	72	$0	$4,652,103	$7,590,000
23	73	$0	$4,960,028	$7,793,812
24	74	$0	$5,283,669	$8,115,232
25	75	$0	$5,626,077	$8,452,160
26	76	$0	$5,990,627	$8,808,331
27	77	$0	$6,376,122	$9,181,048
28	78	$0	$6,783,988	$9,571,488
29	79	$0	$7,215,415	$9,981,548
30	80	$0	$7,670,568	$10,412,102
31	81	$0	$8,154,071	$10,870,117
32	82	$0	$8,664,444	$11,353,027
33	83	$0	$9,203,386	$12,402,979
34	84	$0	$9,772,396	$12,971,587
35	85	$0	$10,373,085	$13,570,073
36	86	$0	$11,005,688	$14,197,860
37	87	$0	$11,699,207	$14,856,348
38	88	$0	$12,364,170	$15,548,974
39	89	$0	$13,093,056	$16,272,966
40	90	$0	$14,647,039	$17,028,840

"Fred, at all times you have full access to your cash value. The cash value can be accessed either by withdrawals or loans. I won't go into the technicalities of either at this point, but you have complete access to it at all times. Fred, what kind of cash value is the illustration showing at age 71?"

"It looks like about $4,377,911," he replied.

"That's right. And by comparison you would have had $4,376,400 in the mutual fund. The life insurance actually gives you more liquidity than you would have had in the mutual fund investment, even though the policy is earning less on a gross basis. This is because no taxes are coming out of your growth in the life insurance policy."

I continued, "Fred, if you were to die at age 71, how much would your wife and kids get from the life insurance policy?" I asked.

"It looks like a little over $7.5 million," he observed.

"And by comparison, your wife and kids would have only received $4,367,00 if you had your money in the mutual fund.

"Follow the illustration down to age 80," I instructed. "What is the cash value and death benefit at that point?"

"It looks like I would have cash value of nearly $7.7 million, and the death benefit would be about $10.4 million."

"And by comparison" I added "at that point you would have had a mutual fund balance of about $6.3 million. The life insurance gives you almost $1.5 more in living value and about $4 million more in death benefit!"

"Let's take this out to age 90," I continued. "How much cash value would you be able to get your hands on?"

"Over $14.5 million," Fred responded.

"And what is the death benefit at that point?" I asked.

"A little more than $17 million," he replied.

"Had you invested in the mutual fund at age 90, you would have had only about $9.5 million," I concluded.

"Fred, you'll notice that the cash value in the life insurance outpaces the growth in the mutual fund we were discussing, even though the interest earnings in the life insurance are assumed to be less. This is because there are no taxes with life insurance. I don't mean to suggest that there are no fees associated with the protection. The insurance company takes fees out every month to cover the insurance cost. But the fees that are coming out in the insurance policy are far less than the fees and taxes that would come out of a mutual fund investment."

"Where does it show the fees that the insurance company is charging?" Fred asked.

"It's not explicitly shown on the illustration," I explained. "But there is a convenient way of calculating them." I took out my financial calculator. "Here's how it works out. If I were able to grow $4.2 million at 7% annually without any fees or taxes, it would grow to about $16.25 million over 20 years. But in year 20, the policy does not have $16.25 million in cash value; it only has about $14.5 million. What that means is that over 20 years the insurance charges have been about $1.75 million."

"I knew there was a catch!" Fred exclaimed.

"Well the insurance company cannot work for free. But what you need to compare this to is the money that you would have otherwise paid in taxes and fees," I explained. "You'll recall that the taxes and fees on the mutual fund over 20 years totaled about $5 million."

"Also," I added, "at age 90 the death benefit is about $2.5 million more than the cash value and about $7 million more than what you would have had in the mutual fund. So the insurance charges are more than covered when you die."

Fred scratched his head. "I guess I would rather pay $1.75 million in charges to the insurance company than $5 million in taxes."

"Another benefit for you," I added "is that you mentioned not handling market volatility well. One nice thing about equity indexed universal life is that your cash value will never be depleted by market crashes. The mutual fund portfolio that we discussed would likely take losses from time to time, especially with 2/3 in equities. Bonds, by the way, can take losses too. The life insurance cash value, on the other hand, is guaranteed to earn at least 2% each year."

"Fred," I continued. "Let's go back to what your stated objectives were with your investments and compare which product does a better job of meeting your objectives."

"You said that your main goal was to grow your

money," I said. "And the life insurance actually grows more quickly than the mutual fund under the realistic assumptions that we made. We'll chalk one up for life insurance. Your second objective was to maintain access to your money and, here, life insurance wins again. Not only will you have more money to access but it is actually more liquid than the mutual fund."

"How do you figure it is more liquid?" Fred challenged.

"The mutual fund portfolio that we've been discussing is likely to go up and down with the market," I said. "From 2000 to 2002 the market lost about 50% of its value. It then recovered over the next several years and saw a correction of about 40% in 2008. The blended portfolio we've been discussing probably would not have such dramatic swings, but it would not be immune to losses in the 15%-20% range," I added.

"What does that have to do with liquidity?" Fred asked.

"Suppose something came up and you needed $1,000,000. All of your money is in mutual funds, and they happen to be down 20% at the time you need the money. How would you feel about withdrawing from your funds?" I asked.

"That would probably be the worst time to liquidate," Fred replied.

"And what if that need came up in a good year when your funds were up 30%?" I prodded.

"I guess it would bother me to take money out when I'm on a roll," he said.

"People never have this problem with life insurance," I said with a smile. "Your cash value is always there for you in whatever market conditions exist. I think you'll agree that the life insurance policy wins in the liquidity area as well."

"Let's move on to taxes and insurance premiums," I added. "With the life insurance I proposed, you wouldn't be paying any ongoing premiums out of pocket, but the insurance company will take fees out of the cash value like we covered. The good news is that there are no taxes when properly structured. By comparison, the mutual fund will incur both taxes and investment advisory fees, which are much greater than the insurance charges. Again, I think you would need to call life insurance the winner in this category."

"Finally," I concluded, "you wanted your wife and kids to get as much as possible when you die as long as it doesn't interfere with your previously stated goals. I think I have shown that it does not interfere with those objectives, and clearly we are leaving much more of an inheritance with life insurance!"

"Well, that sounds like a good deal," Fred remarked. "But why couldn't I just buy a term policy now and if I wanted to do a big single premium policy 20 years from now do the universal life at that time?"

"I'm glad you asked that," I replied. "There are a couple of reasons why that won't work. For one thing, you might not be healthy enough to qualify 20 years from now. Secondly, the tax code does not permit you to make such a large premium into a policy that early. The reason why this worked in our case is that we had 20 years to allow the policy to build a capacity to hold more premium. Finally, policies are heavily laden with fees and expenses in the early years. That's why the Bedrock UL policy has such meager value in the early years. By the time you are ready to put big money in the Bedrock policy, most of the big fees and charges have worked themselves out of the policy."

"This is a lot to contemplate. And Suze would have a fit if I put that kind of money into a life insurance policy," Fred pondered aloud.

"Then Suze must not share our distain for income taxes," I quipped.

"Keep in mind, you don't need to decide to fund the policy this way now," I told Fred. "That decision can be made down the road, and you'll have 20 years to decide. But in order to have this option, you need to have the universal life policy in place now."

This, by far, is the most attractive "exit strategy" of universal life.

Chapter 9

Benefit 7: The Almost Ultimate Tax Haven

"We are taxed twice as much by our idleness,
three times as much by our pride and four times
as much by our foolishness."
Benjamin Franklin

"Fred, I know the idea of plowing a ton of money into a life insurance policy probably flies in the face of everything you've been led to believe about finance," I admitted. "And I don't expect you to be sold on that idea today. Hopefully, over the next 20 years of us working together, you will become more comfortable with the immense benefits of using life insurance in the way I described," I said. But, then again, maybe you won't. For those who can't get comfortable with the idea of super-funding a policy like I just described, there is an alternative tax savings strategy that both you and Suze Boreman would find attractive. I call it the Almost Ultimate Tax Haven," I explained.

"This strategy is spelled out in section 1035 of the tax code, which covers like kind exchanges," I told

Fred. "Are you familiar with the concept of like kind exchanges?"

"I've heard of them in real estate," Fred answered. "If you sell a piece of real estate at a profit, you don't have to pay capital gains taxes as long as you buy a new property for a greater price."

"With real estate, that is called a 1031 exchange," I said. "And your description is partially correct. In reality, you do not avoid the capital gain tax; you just push it off until later, when you sell the replacement asset. The tax code allows us to do these types of exchanges with life insurance and annuities. Section 1035 allows you to swap one life insurance policy for another life insurance policy or swap an annuity for a new annuity or a life insurance policy to an annuity," I explained to Fred. "And when you do this, you defer the tax treatment until the replacement asset is liquidated.

"With the almost ultimate tax haven strategy," I continued, "you will use a 1035 exchange to swap your life insurance policy for an annuity. By doing this, your cost basis in the life insurance policy will become the cost basis in the annuity, and the cash value of the life insurance policy will become your account value in the annuity," I said.

"Why would I want to do that?" Fred asked.

"There would not be any gain in my life insurance policy if it only had a surrender value of $140,000. I could just take the $140,000 tax free right? What tax would I be avoiding?"

"The most common reason somebody would want to do a 1035 exchange of a life insurance policy into an annuity would be to defer the tax when there is a gain in the life insurance contract," I explained. "Most people never consider the benefits of using an exchange when the life insurance policy is 'under water'; that is when the cash value is less than the premiums paid.

"Fred, suppose you had purchased the Bedrock universal life and paid 20 premiums of $42,000," I continued. "Your cost basis in the life insurance policy would be $840,000, and it would have $140,000 of cash value. If you exchanged your life insurance policy for an annuity, you would have an annuity with $140,000 of value and a cost basis of $840,000," I explained further. "Your $140,000 could grow in value to $840,000 before you had to pay a single penny of income tax. You would completely avoid all taxes on up to $700,000 of growth!"

"How do you expect that I can grow $140,000 to $840,000 in my lifetime?" asked Fred. "Remember, I will be 70 year old at the time. How long do you expect me to live?!"

"You probably won't be able to turn $140,000 into $840,000," I responded. "But do think you could turn $2 million into $2.7 million, or $3 million into $3.7 million?"

"Sure, I guess, probably in a couple of years," Fred answered. "But where are you getting those numbers?"

"Suppose you exchanged your life insurance policy for an annuity," I explained. "You would have an annuity with $140,000 of value and a cost basis of $840,000. Instead of investing the full $4.2 million from the sale of your business into taxable mutual funds, suppose you took $2 million and added that into the annuity. You would then have an annuity with $2,140,000 account value and a cost basis of $2,840,000. Now you will be able to grow the annuity to $2,840,000 before you had to pay any income tax," I said. "It is almost as if you've conferred the tax benefits of the life insurance policy onto your mutual funds.

"Once the account reaches its cost basis, you can take out all of the money tax free and invest it however you see fit, or you could just leave it in the annuity where it will continue to grow tax deferred," I added. "But any growth beyond the

$2,840,000 basis will eventually be taxed when you take the money out."

"What if I never take the money out?" Fred asked.

"When you die, the money will pass to the named beneficiaries, and they will have to pay tax on any growth above your cost basis," I answered. "Unlike other assets, annuities do not receive a step up in basis at death. Let's assume that you did this, you died with $3 million in the annuity and it had a cost basis of $2,840,000. If your two children were named as the beneficiary," I said, "the children would receive the full $3 million, and each would pay income tax on the $80,000 of growth.

"The reason I call this the Almost Ultimate Tax Haven is that, while life insurance is completely income tax free, the annuity is taxable to the extent the value exceeds the basis."

"But couldn't I invest the money from the sale of the business into annuities even if I did not buy the universal life policy?" Fred asked.

"Sure you could, but you would not get the benefit of having the increased cost basis, which allows for the tax-free growth," I responded. "Without having the cost basis of the life insurance policy, all of your annuity's earnings would at some point become taxable.

"Even though the tax advantages of this strategy are much smaller than the life insurance strategy that we discussed earlier, they are still quite substantial," I continued. "The annuity strategy allows you to escape income tax on about $700,000 of investment earnings. Assuming a 40% tax bracket, that amounts to income tax savings of almost $300,000.

"Fred, again, after accounting for the cash surrender value, the Bedrock universal life costs about $2,000 per year more than the term policy," I explained further. "Knowing that the universal life will save nearly $300,000 in income taxes should make this a really easy decision. Where else would you be able to invest $2,000 per year for 20 years to get back $300,000?" I asked.

I added, "Suze may not even have an objection to this as you could even invest the annuity with her. But you will probably need to teach her this trick yourself since she is obviously not well versed in the benefits of permanent life insurance."

Chapter 10

Benefit 8: Tax Deductible Life Insurance???

Worried about an IRS audit? Avoid what's called
a red flag. That's something the IRS always looks
for. For example, say you have some money left
in your bank account after paying taxes.
That's a red flag.
Jay Leno

For some reason, this benefit is the one that gets
the most attention—both from clients and advisors to whom I tell about the strategy. Oddly, its
economic value is not as great as some of the previous exit strategies we've discussed and, in practice, it is the most complicated. But for some reason, a tax deduction has more "sex appeal" than
tax-free growth.

I continue with my conversation with Fred.

"Fred, suppose you bought the Bedrock policy.
We'll assume that you never missed a premium
payment and never benefitted from the lapse protection feature," I said. "We'll also assume that you

never triggered a long-term care benefit. Further we'll assume that you never utilized any of the exit strategies I've outlined so far. Before cashing in that policy, you need to know about one more benefit. How would you like to get a tax deduction for your life insurance premiums?" I asked.

"I wish I could, but my accountant says there is no way to deduct these premiums," responded Fred.

"Technically your accountant is right," I said. "Premiums for life insurance, even when the insurance is required for business purposes, are not tax deductible. But there is a way to indirectly take a deduction for almost all of the premiums you pay for a universal life policy, and you cannot do this with term," I explain. "You don't get the deduction right away; you get it after the insurance is no longer needed. And it only applies if you don't elect any of the other exit strategies we discussed."

"How does it work?" Fred asked.

"Over 20 years, the Bedrock universal life policy will cost $840,000 in premiums and at the end of 20 years, it will have $140,000 of cash value," I explained. "Where did the remaining $700,000 go?" I asked.

"I guess that was the cost of the insurance."

"Exactly," I said. "And you can get a tax deduction for that amount, but only with universal life, not term insurance. If we viewed life insurance like an investment we would say that the Bedrock universal policy had a large loss," I explained. "We paid $840,000 for something that is worth only $140,000. The IRS does not recognize that as a loss, however, because the 'lost' money was used to pay for the life insurance protection, which is not deductible. But here's how we can take the loss," I explained. "Like with the 'almost ultimate tax haven' strategy, we exchange the life insurance policy for an annuity, but we do not add any additional money. We now have an annuity with $140,000 and a cost basis of $840,000. While losses inside a life insurance policy are not deductible, losses in annuity contracts are deductible," I added.

Fred nodded.

"Suppose your $140,000 annuity grows in value to $150,000, and you decide then to cash it in," I continued. "You are entitled to take a loss on your taxes for the difference between the basis and the amount received. In this case, the loss would be $690,000," I said.

"Could I just buy the annuity and cash it in the next day?" Fred asked cleverly.

"Probably not," I answered. "The loss is only allowed if you purchased the annuity with the goal of making money," I cautioned. "Nobody would ever buy an annuity for one day and expect to make any money. The IRS would claim that you obviously had no profit motive and it was just a tax ploy. There is no statutory time frame for how long you need to hold the annuity before cashing it in, but it needs to be reasonable. I would recommend holding on to the annuity for a couple of years and get some growth before cashing it in. Ideally, you should wait until any surrender charges have gone away or at least wait until your earnings are greater than the surrender charges," I said.

"The other thing to keep in mind is that you need to have taxable income that is greater than the loss you are taking because the loss cannot be carried forward," I told Fred. "For this reason I normally suggest my clients divide the exchange between several different annuities so that they could be surrendered at different times, just to make sure that we are not leaving any money on the table."

"And this is all okay with the IRS?" Fred asked.

"There is no question on whether the deduction is allowed, but there is some disagreement as to where on the 1040 the deduction is to be taken, and the tax code is not clear on where it should be taken," I explained. "The IRS has taken the position that it should be taken on Schedule A as a 'miscellaneous' deduction. But all other investment-related losses are taken on the first page of the 1040, and some accountants want to take it there," I added.

"What's the difference between the two, as long as I am able to take the deduction?" Fred asked.

"Many of the deductions that are taken on schedule A are only deductible to the extent that they exceed 2% of your adjusted gross income," I responded. "For instance, if your adjusted gross income it $200,000, and you take a $100,000 loss on Schedule A, you are only allowed a deduction of $96,000 because $4,000 (2% of $200,000) is not deductible."

"That doesn't sound like a big difference between taking a $100,000 deduction or a $96,000 deduction," Fred said. "Why not just do it the way the IRS wants us to?"

"It gets a bit more complicated," I answered. "If you are subject to the alternative minimum tax (AMT), and you take the deduction on schedule A subject to the 2% threshold, you may lose the value of the deduction due to the application of the AMT," I explained. "It is possible to manipulate your timing on when certain income is received and certain expenses are paid so that you would be able to escape the AMT in certain years. If your CPA plans on taking the deduction on Schedule A subject to the 2% threshold, you would want to liquidate the annuity in a year that AMT would not apply. And you may want to 'engineer' your income in a way to avoid the AMT.

"It is also possible that the deduction could be taken on Schedule A and not be subject to the 2% threshold," I explained further. "In this case, you would benefit from the deduction even if you were subject to the AMT. The tax benefits of taking it on Schedule A not subject to the threshold are the same as taking it on page 1 of the 1040.

"Fred, between your Social Security, distributions from your retirement plans, and income you receive from the sale of your business, it is very clear that you will be in the top tax bracket, would you agree?" I asked.

"I imagine I would," he answered.

"Today, the top tax bracket is around 50% in most states, and even higher in some states," I stated.

"I thought the top bracket was 39.6%," Fred said.

"That is currently the top bracket for federal income tax, but there is an additional tax of 3.8% that applies to investment income for high earners, nicknamed the Obamacare Tax," I explained. "On top of that, you have state income taxes, which in our state is about 6%. Add those together and it's right around 50%.

"If you were able to take a $690,000 tax deduction in a 50% bracket it would save you $345,000 on your income taxes for that year.

"Again, the net cost of the Bedrock universal life policy is only $2,000 per year more than the term," I reminded him. "If you knew that by spending this additional premium now would save you $345,000 in the future, wouldn't you do it?" I asked.

Chapter 11

Income Taxes

The difference between death and taxes is death doesn't get worse every time Congress meets.
Will Rogers

"Fred, let's change the subject a little bit from money and insurance and talk about what's going on in the country right now," I said. "What do you think are the biggest challenges our country faces?"

"Well, we definitely need to get the economy back on track," he answered. "And we have to get control of our spending. Social Security is destined to go broke, as is Medicare, not to mention our spiraling national debt," he added wryly. "And who knows what will happen with health care."

"I agree. And, eventually, we will fix these problems because we have no other choice, or our country will not survive. There are really only two ways to fix our financial house. We can either reduce spending or increase revenue. Time and time again we hear politicians talking about reducing spending, cleaning up waste, etc. But, year after year, we always end up spending more than the year before. In the end, they always find it easier to raise taxes," I said.

"Fred, in light of the economic challenges our country faces, do you think that tax rate will be higher or lower in the future?" I asked.

"My guess would be higher," he responded. "But, as you said earlier, the top tax rate is now about 50%. How much higher can it go?"

"The answer might surprise you," I responded. "Look at the chart below. Did you know that in 1962 the top federal bracket was 92%? The top bracket for the rest of the 1960s and 1970s was 70%. Reagan lowered it to 28%, and it has gradually risen since. While a 50% tax rate seems high today, it is actually fairly low by historical standards," I explained.

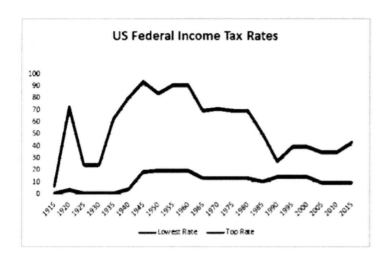

"The reason I bring this up," I added, "is that we have no idea what tax rates will be in the future, and there is very little we can do to control the overall tax rates in the country, but we can do things to control our own tax rates.

"A lot of the advantages of universal life that we've been discussing are tax advantages," I said. "Suppose that income tax rates rose to the 70% level that we experienced in the 60s and 70s. Would the advantages of universal life be better or worse under the higher tax scenario?" I asked Fred.

"I guess those advantages would be magnified," he answered.

"One thing I've learned from my clients over the years is that when it comes to building substantial wealth it's not because of a single investment or a single strategy," I said. "The people who build great wealth tend to have very flexible financial plans to allow them to deal with the uncertainties in life. I think I've made an excellent case that universal life offers a lot of flexibility to capitalize on opportunities—from lapse protection to long-term care benefits and an array of exit strategies. The slight additional cost of the universal life policy is very small compared to the benefits it provides," I explained.

I could see Fred understood.

"I'm sure that you've learned a lot, but I know that some of this will need to sink in," I told Fred. "What I think we should do is apply to both Boulder Life and Bedrock Life. Underwriting will take several weeks, which will give you time to think about it. We can put off making a decision until the insurance companies have come back with offers," I suggested.

"Okay, but you said that universal life has eight advantages other than cash value," Fred pointed out. "You've only covered seven. What is the eighth?"

"Not everybody is eligible for the eighth benefit," I answered. "I will know if you are eligible in a couple of weeks. If it applies to you we can discuss it later. Meanwhile, I've given you enough to chew on," I said with a laugh.

Chapter 12

Benefit 9: Table Shave

"I know a man who gave up smoking, drinking,
sex, and rich food. He was healthy right up to
the day he killed himself."
Johnny Carson

Fred, the last time we met I told you that I would
explain the final benefit if you qualify, and you
do," I told him. "But before going into that, what
are your thoughts about the advantages of universal
life based on our discussion?"

"Well, I do see the benefits of what we've discussed," Fred answered. "But it's a lot to wrap my
head around," he admitted. "For instance, I don't
know whether I would be better off by selling the
policy at the end or doing the Ultimate Tax Haven
or the Almost Ultimate Tax Haven strategy."

"There's no need to decide now," I said. "You can
make those decisions later. All you need to decide
now is whether you want to have those options
available to you."

"Maybe I'll do some term and some universal life," Fred said.

"Fred, the final benefit of universal life will make your decision very easy," I told him. "Remember how I said that your health seemed to be border-line for a standard offer?"

"Yes."

"Well, your weight was about 10 pounds high-er than you reported to me," I told him. "Your cholesterol and blood pressure were also slightly higher. And, your blood sugar is in the pre-diabet-ic range. Boulder Life came back with a table four offer, which means their premium is double what I quoted. I called my underwriter at Dinosaur Life and he said that based on your conditions they would be at three tables at an annual premium of $52,000. The Granite City underwriter said that they would also be at three tables and slightly high-er in premium than Dinosaur. So it looks like the best premium available for 20-year term is about $52,000," I explained.

"Fred, a lot of companies have what we call a ta-ble shave program, where they issue standard rates for people who would otherwise be rated," I ex-plained further. "Since universal life is normally purchased with a longer time horizon than term, and because the premium is normally much higher, the insurance company can afford to be more flexible in underwriting. The companies that offer these programs normally forgive between two tables and four tables," I said. "Bedrock does have a table shave program, and they allow up to three tables."

"What was their offer?" Fred asked.

"Technically, it was four tables, but they were able to apply some credits based on the fact that you exercise regularly," I said. "Those credits got you down to three tables, and you qualify for the table shave program. That means there is no change to the premium I quoted for the Bedrock universal life. All the additional advantages, including cash value, long-term care benefit, continuability, salability, Ultimate Tax Haven, Almost Ultimate Tax Haven, and potential for tax deduction, will apply to you at a premium even less than term.

"Fred, my recommendation would be to take the full $10 million with the Bedrock universal life. What do think?" I asked.

"Tom, what are you waiting for? Sign me up!" Fred exclaimed finally.

Appendix

Case Study

Acme Manufacturing is a manufacturer of products used in the home building trade. It was started by father and son, Ken and Ron Jones, who each own 50% of the shares. Acme was profitable but they badly needed capital to expand into new markets. My client, Dennis Anderson, had a history of turning around troubled companies and growing already profitable companies. In 2004 Dennis bought 34% of the stock, with Ken and Ron each having 33% ownership. Given Dennis' strong banking relationships, excellent reputation, and strong personal balance sheet, the company was able to borrow the much needed capital to expand their operations.

When Dennis joined Acme, he was 70 years old, and the market value of the company was about $8 million. His plan was to aggressively grow the company over the next several years and sell out at age 75. He was hoping to grow the market value to $18 million.

One of the first things Dennis did after buying

in was to implement a buy-sell agreement. The agreement stipulated that if any of the partners die, the surviving partners would purchase the descedent's shares at a predetermined price formula. To set this in motion, they purchased $6 million of life insurance on each partner. The life insurance proceeds would first be used to retire the new debt that the company took on for its expansion plans, with the remainder to be used to purchase shares of the deceased shareholder. It was anticipated that all debt would be retired within Dennis' five-year plan at which time each shareholder's stock would be worth about $6 million each.

Given Dennis' age, his life insurance was the most expensive. The policy they purchased on Dennis was a 10-year level term for $6 million with an annual premium of $87,200. Dennis' policy was convertible only to age 75. After the 10-year level premium period, the policy's annual premium would rise to over $800,000 and increase each year after that. Dennis was not worried about the increasing premiums at age 80, since he did not anticipate keeping the policy after he sold out.

Ken, age 55 at the time of the application, took out a 15-year term policy at a premium of $17,158 level to age 70. After age 70, Ken's premium would increase to $305,468 and continue to increase each year. The policy was convertible to universal life for the entire 15-year period up to age 70. Based on the company's current line of universal life policy, the annual premium required to convert at age 70 is $242,300 to hold the policy to age 100.

Ken's son, Ron, had a history of bladder cancer. The cancer was a fairly low grade and he was cancer free five years post treatment. He received a four-table rating. In addition he used chewing tobacco, which classifies him as a tobacco user with most companies. Knowing that his cancer could always return, Dennis and Ken wanted to be sure that Ron was able to keep his life insurance as long as possible. Their agent had suggested universal life, but they found the premiums to be too high. They opted for a 30-year term policy at a premium of $47,345.

Ron was 33 at the time of issue. The premium for his term policy would increase to $531,425 at age 63 and increase each year thereafter. The policy was convertible to universal life for the entire 30-year duration. The cost to convert to universal life at age 63 would be $476,000 to keep the policy in force to age 100.

Acme Manufacturing Existing Term Policies					
$6,000,000 each					
Insured	Issue Age	Issue Class	Term Length	Current Premium	Conversion Premium
Dennis	70	Standard	10	$87,200	$817,200
Ken	55	Pref.	15	$17,154	$242,300
Ron	33	Tobacco T4	30	$47,345	$476,000
			Total	$151,699	

The first several years following Dennis' investment were great years. The company was able to secure large lines of credit, which allowed them to open new plants and expand into new markets. Sales were skyrocketing. Then the financial crisis hit.

In 2008 the mortgage crisis brought the economy to its knees. The homebuilding industry was especially hard hit. In addition to reduced sales revenue, Acme had a growing list of receivables, which were further hampering the company. Acme went into survival mode. It was evident to Dennis that he would not be able to reach his goals and sell out at age 75. He had to stay in a little bit longer.

After a few years, the company had survived the financial crisis and things were beginning to get back on track. Dennis was now 77, and he began discussing plans to sell his shares to his partners. They were enthusiastic about buying Dennis' shares, assuming they could get financing.

The three partners met with their bankers to arrange the financing for the buyout.

The banker greeted them, "Dennis, good to see you again. I've had a chance to review your balance sheet and income statement. Congratulations, it looks like you made it through that downturn. I know things were tough for a while."

"So the point of this meeting," he continued is to discuss financing your partners buying out your shares?"

"Yes," Dennis replied, "we've really built up the company and I am ready to take my chips off the table."

"Well," replied that banker, "lending has gotten a lot stricter since we last spoke about financing. I see a couple of challenges. First of all, the company currently has a little over $3 million in debt, which is backed by your personal guarantee. Dennis, if you are no longer with the company, I doubt you will want to continue to guarantee the loans."

"Can't you take a personal guarantee from my partners?" Dennis asked.

"We could," replied the banker, "if their personal balance sheets are strong enough to guarantee the loans. But it looks like most of their net worth is either in the business itself or in retirement plans. I'm afraid that we won't be able to lend additional money. And if you leave the company, we may even call the existing loans. Ten years ago, we would probably have done this, but 2008 really changed the way banks operate," the banker said in an apologetic tone.

Dennis continued talking to other bankers only to hear the same story. Dennis knew that his involvement in the business would continue for at least a few more years. He was now age 77 and the three remaining years on his term policy was now a major concern. If he would still be involved as a partner in the business after age 80, there would be no life insurance to execute the buy-sell agreement. And his family would likely never receive the full value of his interest when he died.

Dennis called his insurance agent to explore his options. The term policy was no longer convertible but Dennis was still in good health. A new 10-year term policy for $6 million would cost about $250,000 a year. The agent also suggested a five-year term policy but the premium was not significantly lower. Neither of the term policies was convertible, and there was a good possibility of

Dennis outliving the coverage.

Dennis discussed his dilemma with his attorney. The attorney suggested that he call me.

I met with Dennis and explained all the advantages of universal life versus term for all of the partners. In terms of Dennis' coverage, the universal life could be kept in force for as long as he needed it, whether it was three more years or 30 more years.

I designed a policy for Dennis that would provide $6 million of coverage for three more years at a premium of $125,000. This was about $38,000 more than his existing policy, but the policy could be continued into the fourth year, if needed, at a premium of about $150,000. A fifth year of coverage would have cost about $165,000. While the premiums were higher than what he had now, the cost of extending coverage was, by far, more affordable.

Even though the premiums were higher, I explained how the "back end" benefits more than justified the higher premiums. Dennis was very wealthy and he knew that he had more money than he would ever be able to spend in his life. His goal at this point in his life was to leave a large inheritance for his children and grandchildren. He saw life insurance as an ideal tool to accomplish that goal.

"Dennis," I said, "what I proposed will meet your goals and give you several more benefits that you weren't expecting, but the premium will be about $38,000 more. However, I found a way to lessen the blow of the increased premium."

"What's that?" he asked.

"The company I quoted has a table shave program where they allow four tables at standard rates. You qualified for standard on your own so this was no benefit to you. But right now Ron is being charged with four tables. He qualifies as a standard risk on their universal life policies. Even better, this company will allow tobacco chewers to qualify for non-smoker rates. Believe it or not, I am able to cut Ron's premium by about 50% on a universal life policy. That savings will go a long way to off-set the increase in your own policy."

"Will Ron's policy develop any cash value?" Dennis asked.

"It could if we paid the same as what he was pay-ing on his term" I replied. "But I figured you were more interested in keeping the premium low. I solved for the required premium to carry the pol-icy for at least as long as his term was going to run, and the premium on the universal life was still quite a bit lower. What's really great is that Ron will get all the 'other benefits' of universal life. This is especially important because if Ron's cancer comes back he could continue this coverage at much more affordable rates."

"And what about Ken?" asked Dennis.

"Ken's term policy was really cheap," I replied. "And I wasn't able to beat it with universal life. The closest I was able to come was about $8,000 more than term you have on him. But I did find out that Ken was thinking about buying a long-term care policy at a premium of $5,000 a year. Since the universal life that I quoted contains a long-term care benefit, I suppose that he could use the life insurance instead and he could save that $5,000 expense."

The following chart shows the proposed universal life policies:

Proposed IUL Acme Manufacturing			
$6,000,000 each			
Insured	**Issue Age**	**Issue Class**	**Proposed Premium***
Dennis	77	Standard	$125,200
Ken	62	Pref.	$25,154
Ron	40	Standard	$24,250
		Total:	$174,604

*Premium required to match coverage duration of existing term policies.

In this case, the premiums for the indexed UL were approximately 15% more than what they were paying for term and it solved Dennis' problem of being able to continue the coverage if he was not able to sell out by the time his term expired. It also allowed Ron and Ken much more affordable options to continue their coverage instead of converting the term policies.

Insured	Conversion Premium to age 100	Premium to Continue UL to age 100	Yearly Savings
Dennis	$817,200	$273,000	$544,200
Ken	$242,300	$89,000	$153,300
Ron	$476,000	$138,000	$338,000

"The universal life is clearly the best option for both me and Ron," Dennis said. "And we can't really do that for ourselves without doing the same for Ken so let's do it for all three of us."

It has now been almost three years since I sold these policies. Acme has continued to grow and they just finished their best year ever. Dennis has found a bank willing to finance the buyout and is now planning on selling out his interest for about $7,000,000.

Dennis is planning on using $2.5 million to fund the "Ultimate Tax Haven" strategy that I outlined in an earlier chapter.

Life Insurance in Retirement
Tom Martin CFP®,CLU®,ChFC®

Most financial pundits in the media scorn the idea of having life insurance in retirement. Their rationale seems to make sense of the surface: Life insurance is designed to replace your earnings when you die. Once you retire (and have no earnings) you are living off your investments. When you die, your investments don't die with you, so what is the purpose of using valuable funds to pay for unneeded coverage?

Life insurance clearly plays an important role for very wealthy clients to efficiently transfer their estate, but are the media pundits correct in their advice for the average family to dump their coverage? Probably not.

Let's consider the following statistics:

• The average American approaching retirement has retirement assets to replace only 10% of his/her pre-retirement earnings.

• 55% of Americans over age 65 rely on Social Security to provide over half of their income.

• The maximum monthly Social Security retirement benefit for a person reaching full retirement age in 2015 is $2,642.

These statistics clearly show that Social Security
is a vital source of retirement income. When we
view our Social Security benefits statements we
tend to discount the importance of this benefit
as benefits are expressed in "today's dollars." In
reality, our actual benefits will be much larger due
to inflation. By contrast, when we consider how
much savings we will have at retirement, we often
fail to consider that the values of those dollars will
be similarly reduced due to inflation. Consider the
following example.

John and Jane Doe, age 50 and 45 respectively,
plan on working to John's full retirement age of
67. John is making $150,000 per year and Mary
earns $70,000 per year. John and Jane both con-
tribute to a 401k plan and, based on their investment assumptions, they figure that they will have
$1,000,000 in retirement funds by the time John
reaches age 67. Assuming a 5% withdrawal rate,
they will be able to withdraw about $50,000 per
year.

John receives his Social Security statement and
sees that his retirement benefit will be the maxi-

mum, which is $2,642 in today's dollars. Jane's benefit is projected to be $1,450 if she claims at age 62 (same year John retires). John and Jane falsely assume that Social Security will provide about half of their retirement income, which is $49,000 from Social Security and $50,000 from retirement accounts.

In reality, both will receive much larger Social Security checks since these amounts will be indexed for inflation. If we assume 3% inflation, John's actual benefit will be about $77,000 per year and Jane's will be about $40,000 per year. In reality, despite a respectful retirement account balance, Social Security will actually provide about 70% of their income.

Since Social Security benefits continue to increase with inflation, by the time John is age 80, his Social Security benefit will have risen to $113,000 at which point Jane's benefit will be about $59,000. Let's assume that John dies at age 80 and Jane lives to age 85. At John's death Jane will assume John's benefit and lose her own benefit. The total Social Security benefit will drop by $59,000 per year. Since Jane will spend 10 years as a widow, this loss amounts to $590,000!

Even though they have a sizable retirement account, it only represents about 30% of their income. Such a substantial reduction in Social Security benefits is likely to cause a substantial reduction in Jane's lifestyle.

The financial pundits would be quick to recommend that John purchases a term policy today to cover his "temporary" insurance need. They figure that once John retires, he has no earnings to protect. In reality, his death after retirement will cause a substantial reduction in household income. John should consider some form of permanent insurance for at least part of his insurance portfolio in order to mitigate the eventual loss of the Social Security benefit. If Jane predeceases John, John would lose Jane's benefit. Even if the permanent insurance was just on John's life, he could still utilize his policy to replace the benefit he lost on Jane. He could use the policy to provide a tax-free income stream through withdrawals and loans. He could cash the policy in, replace it with an annuity or even sell the policy as a life settlement.

In summary, life insurance can play a critical role in helping couples meet their retirement goals whether it be through utilization of the policy's cash value or in having the death benefit replace the lost social security benefit.

ARE CAPS AND FLOORS IN IULS REALISTIC, AND IF SO, WHY CAN'T I DO THIS MYSELF?

By: Thomas M. Martin, CFP®, ChFC®, CLU®

We are often asked by our clients "how can the insurance company afford such generous caps and floors in their indexed universal life policies?" Many insurance producers themselves may ponder the same question. We may even take it a step further and wonder if the insurance company can do this in a life insurance policy, shouldn't we be able to do this in our own investment portfolios without the insurance fees associated with the policy. Before addressing the latter, we need to understand how the insurance company hedges to be able to offer their stated caps and floors.

As an example, we'll assume XYZ insurance company offers an indexed universal life with a one-year point-to-point crediting strategy on the S&P 500, a 0% floor, and a 12% cap with a 100% participation rate. So if a policy begins the year with $100,000 of account value, it is guaranteed to end the year with at least $100,000 in account value and possibly up to $112,000 (less insurance charges and policy fees in both cases).

Now, let's assume that XYZ has a general fund that they know will earn 5.5% interest this year (which is about the industry average). The insurance company would need to have $94,787 of your $100,000 invested in their general fund at 5.5% in order to guarantee your $100,000 account balance at your policy anniversary. This leaves them with $5,213 to invest in an option strategy to credit the upside potential of the market. The insurance company uses call options to credit the excess interest.

A call option is a security that gives the purchaser the right to buy a security at a specific price (strike price) within a certain time period. Since this policy is linked to the S&P 500, the insurance company will buy call options on an ETF that mirrors the S&P 500. Spiders (SPY) is one such ETF.

At the time of writing this article, SPY is trading at $200. If the S&P index rises 10%, shares of SPY will also rise 10% to $220 ($20x 1.1%). Since the insurance company will need to credit at least some interest if the S&P index rises at all, they need to buy one-year call options with a strike price equal to the current price of the underlying security. This is called an "on the money call." As long as the index is up by year end, these options will be "in the money." The insurance company will liquidate the options and order to credit excess interest to the policy. If the S&P index falls, the options will be worthless, but the money that was put in the insurance company's general account will now be worth $100,000.

Currently the price of a one-year on-the-money call on SPY is $13.22. This means that for a premium of $13.22 the purchaser will have the right to purchase one share of SPY at a price of $200 until the option expires one year later. If a year from now SPY is trading at $250, the option would be worth $50, as it allows the purchaser a $50 discount to the current price. If the underlying stock is trading at $300, the option would be worth $100. Since there is no limit how high the price of the underlying security may go, the call option offers unlimited profit potential. If the underlying security is trading below the strike price (in this case $200), the option would be worthless and the purchaser would have lost the premium paid.

While the profit potential of a call option is unlimited, the insurance company does not need unlimited profit potential since they are only on the hook to credit your policy up to the cap, in this case 12%. At the time of the call option purchase, the insurance company will also sell an out-of-the-money call option with a strike price higher than the current trading price. Option traders refer to the strategy of buying an on-the-money call and simultaneously selling an out-of-the-money call with both positions having the same expiration date as a "bull call spread." The purpose of using a bull call spread is that the net cost of the option strategy is lower and more options can be purchased. It also caps the upside potential of the position.

A Bull Call Spread consists of one call option purchased on the money and the simultaneous sale of an out-of-the-money call option on the same security with the same expiration date. This strategy caps the potential return of the long position but reduces the net cost of the option.

In our example using a 12% cap, the insurance company will sell call options with a strike price 12% greater than the on-the-money price of $200, in this case, $224. Unfortunately SPY calls are not available at a price of $224, so I will need to round up or round down to come close. In this case I will use a strike price of $225.

Currently a one-year call option on SPY with a strike price of $225 would sell for $2.80. The net cost of the spread will be the price paid for the call purchase (long position) less the price received for selling the call option (short position). In this case, $10.42.

$13.22 (long position)
-$2.80 (short position)
$10.42 Net cost of Spread

As stated earlier, in our example the insurance company has $5,213 available to play the option strategy. At a net cost of $10.42, the insurance company will be able to buy approximately 500 spreads. Let's assume that over the next 12 months the index earns 10%. The insurance company will need to credit your policy with $10,000 of indexed interest. At 10% growth, SPY will be trading at $220 and each 200 call will have an intrinsic value of $20. Since the insurer owns 500 of these call options, their long position is worth $10,000. And since SPY is trading below the short position, the short position will simply expire. In this case, the insurer is perfectly hedged for the caps and floors they are offering.

It is nearly an impossible coincidence that these numbers worked out so perfectly, as I arbitrarily picked the cap, floor, and general account interest rate. In reality, option prices change daily, and if we ran this same analysis a week or a month from now we are likely to get different results. But as long as the strategy comes close, we should have a degree of comfort that the insurance company is not over-promising.

Since all insurers purchase their options at the same exchange and at the same price, how can caps and floors be different amongst different carriers? For instance, suppose ABC is offering a similar policy with a 13% cap, is that insurer over-promising? It may be that the ABC is earning a higher rate in its general account. Suppose ABC has a general account that is earning 6% instead of the 5.5% we assumed with XYZ. ABC would need to have $94,340 of the client's account in the general account, leaving $5,660 available to play the option strategy versus XYZ's $5,213. With more money available for the option strategy, ABC could offer a higher cap or a higher floor or perhaps a combination of both. It is also possible that one company's internal fees and expenses are greater, and the increased fees could also allow more generous rate caps.

Now that we have an understanding of how the insurance companies invest, let's see if we can achieve similar results in our own investment portfolio.

We need to start by finding a safe place to deposit enough of our money so that in one year it will be worth what we started with. In the previous example, the insurance company did this by putting $94,787 in their general account earning 5.5%. Unfortunately, we as individual investors do not have access to such high rates for "safe money." As individual investors, we would probably look for a one-year certificate of deposit or an investment grade zero coupon bond.

At the time of this writing, the highest yield to maturity zero coupon bond with a one-year maturity yields about 2%. Unlike an insurance company, as an individual investor I will have to pay income tax on the 2%. Assuming a tax rate of 40% (federal and state), my net after-tax yield on this 2% bond will be 1.2%. This means that I will need to have $98,814 invested in this bond to have my initial $100,000 one year later. This leaves me with just under $1200 to invest in my call spread strategy in order to participate in the upside of the market.

Assuming I purchased the same bull call spread as the insurance company did in our previous example, I would only be able to afford to purchase 115 options versus the 500 options the insurance company was able buy. Since my option holdings are approximately 1/5 that of the insurance company, my return on the option strategy will be 1/5 that of the insurer. In a year when the insurance policy would have credited 12% interest, my portfolio would have only credited about 2.5%. In a year when the policy would have credited 5%, my portfolio would have only earned about 1%.

Adding insult to injury, my option gains would also be taxable as a short-term gain. Again, assuming a

40% tax rate, my 2.5% and 1% returns would be chopped to 1.5% and .6% respectively.

An astute student of options might suggest an alternate strategy called a collar. A collar strategy is one where the investor buys a security and then buys an equal number of put options with a strike price equal to the price he paid for the underlying stock. The put will then guarantee no loss of principal if the underlying security declines in value. The investor would then sell call options on the underlying security to offset the price of the put.

Let's see if such a strategy would work with SPY. If I started with $100,000, I would be able to purchase 500 shares of SPY at $200 per share. To fully protect my $100,000 investment, I would need to purchase 500 one-year put options at a current price of $15.82. If I were to pay for the puts by selling calls, I would need to find the strike price of a call option approximating the price I paid for the put. Scanning the call option prices, I see that I could sell 195 calls at $16.08 per share. Selling 500 call options would not only pay for the puts, but I would come out about $130 ahead. However, my 500 shares of SPY would be immediately called away at a $5 per share loss, making my net return of the strategy -2.5%.

The bottom line is that after taxes, an individual

investor would not even come close to matching the guarantees and caps of an indexed universal life policy on a gross basis. Keep in mind that gross returns on any life insurance policy will be reduced by the insurance charges and fees charged against it. These fees can vary dramatically from issuer to issuer and are also affected by policy design. Consumers will need to judge for themselves if these fees are justified by the higher gross crediting rates.

Conclusion:

Simply put, permanent life insurance is by far the most flexible and advantageous financial vehicle available. No other investment has the ability to provide a tax-free death benefit, tax-free accumulation, tax-free distributions, and protection for long-term care.

CPSIA information can be obtained at www.ICGtesting.com
Printed in the USA
LVOW12s1107260515

439593LV00002B/3/P